BLOOM ON TILL DOOMSDAY

Poems by

John Norman Price

First published 2023 by IRON Press
5 Marden Terrace
Cullercoats
North Shields
NE30 4PD
tel +44(0)191 2531901
ironpress@xlnmail.com
www.ironpress.co.uk
Find us on Facebook

ISBN 978-1-8383444-2-9
Printed by Imprint Digital

Text © John Norman Price 2023

Cover and book design, Brian Grogan and Peter Mortimer
Typeset in Georgia 11pt

IRON Press books are distributed by IPS UK
and represented by Inpress Ltd
Milburn House, Dean Street
Newcastle upon Tyne NE1 1LF
tel: +44(0)191 2308104
www.inpressbooks.co.uk

Foreword

WRITING POETRY INVOLVES THE CHALLENGE OF TURNING PERSONAL experience into something that has a more general significance. As Don Paterson says in his tome 'The Poem', 'Poems achieve their density...by giving small pieces of information as evidence of larger events, emotions, ideas, domains.' It also involves (for me anyway) a good deal of re-working in order to find the combination of sounds and rhythm that reinforce the meanings.

The actual starting points of the poems in 'Bloom on Till Doomsday' are quite varied. 'Lucky for Some' is based on having seen 'Waiting for Godot' twice and wondering if Lucky's absurd speech is just a cover and in fact he is much more intelligent than he seems.

Simply coming across George Orwell's view that W. B. Yeats was 'an impoverished offshoot of the aristocracy' gave birth to 'Bestowed Upon'.

'She Lives' had a more bizarre beginning. In a pamphlet about looking after a dishwasher it should have said: 'Shelves in the dishwasher...' Instead, it began 'She lives in a dishwasher'. I wrote a few comic lines about a tiny being living off scraps of food but being scrupulously clean. In the end though, the poem I wrote was a deeply felt lament for a lost mother.

Sometimes I needed to do a little research. For 'Angel' I visited the Angel of the North a few times and read about Antony Gormley's thinking, taking special note of this: 'a being that might be more at home in the air, brought down to earth... It is also an image of someone fatally handicapped, who cannot pass through any door and is desperately burdened'. The poems here were written over several years and I owe it to some perceptive editors who have selected and grouped them thematically so that they focus on the human need to bring a sense of purpose to our fragile existence.

John Norman Price

JOHN NORMAN PRICE worked as an English teacher with special interest in drama and film studies before moving into the world of journalism at the Sunderland Echo, where he introduced a national award winning *Newspapers in Education* programme. He has published several media studies books, two novels and short stories. His first IRON Press poetry pamphlet *Bye Bye Blackboard* was published in 2016. John lives with his wife in Washington and has two children and four grandchildren.

The Poems

Thorn Free	7
Angel	8
Lucky for Some	9
Bestowed Upon	11
Leaving	12
Pedlar's Halt	14
She Lives	15
Long Walk Home	16
Lights Out	17
Patient	18
Allotment	20
Kursk	21
Tough Time for Tiresias	23
End Room	26
Sea Rocket	28

Thorn Free

No bed of roses
this new bed of mine.

The petals do not fall
at the first windblast.

It does not demand
to be fed, copiously,
continually.

It has no black spot
galls or cankers.

Its buds do not ball
in the rain.

It is aphid and mildew free.

It does not need
dead-heading.

It is smooth, safe,
thorn free

single.

Angel

"Roots to grow and wings to fly," he said,
then flew south, spawning siblings;
but the roots are tethers and the wings don't work.
Mam called me "Little Angel" but finding me faceless,
lost her faith and sloped back to Hartlepool.
So, as I stand, stranded on this green hill,
people come to gawp, play games around my feet
and though some gaze in awe, most laugh or scorn.

My flights of fancy are my salvation:
free from impediments, I soar among the clouds,
riding thermals, gliding, swooping,
whooping joyfully, laughing at the earthbound
crowds complaining, "We came to see
an angel, not this monstrosity!"

Lucky for Some

I carry his picnic, collapsible chair,
His crutch and corrective whip;
I tolerate his whims, his childish fantasies
And fortify his sense of importance.

It's a steady job, keeps the wolves
From the door, as the saying goes.
I do as he commands, instructs, insists
Because he pays me, not a princely sum

But a sum nevertheless, and I pay no rent.
There have been times though, when I wonder
Why, as, weighed down by his paraphernalia
I protect him as he sleeps on his feet.

But what would he do, left on his own,
With no one to dance a fandango or sing,
Clean his shoes, think his thoughts,
Blow his nose, wipe his large arse?

It's a full life being carer and servant.
Now he is blind I have to be his satnav;
He gives me orders, I give him direction –
The noose round my neck is simply symbolic.

Freedom? Not what it's cracked up to be.
Fathoming the ideas of Cunard and Testew,
Deciphering the insights of Fartov and Belcher,
Playing sports of all sorts, pointlessly?

I will go on doing my duties religiously
So my master and provider may perform
His speeches, gesticulate and pontificate,
Until it's time to shrink and dwindle away.

Bestowed upon

In a far corner of the neglected kitchen garden
of her country house, his small plot hides,
bestowed upon him by her ladyship
in recognition of a former liaison,
though she now attributes her magnanimity
to her love of the arts, for her tamed gardener
is her famous patronised poet. "Take note,"
she tells her touring visitors, "of the neatly trimmed
yew hedge, the lines of beans and the shaven lawn.
Come back in spring and you will see outside
his little cabin door, the host of Ballerina tulips
which remind him of my carefree, dancing days;
then find the same craft and love in his verse."

And when the visitors have marvelled and departed
he sits alone in the wavering shade
of the acacia tree, taking careful note
of the pottering jobs which need attention,
trying to ignore the symbolism of the evening's
purple glow seeping inexorably to his heart's core.

Leaving

Once he knew he was living in extra time
he took off to the tip
with his frozen mower, his dangerous steps
and his rusted saws
leaving his tumbledown shed
in case it might be useful
in the event of a housing crisis.

In the end it was still work in progress
to find homes for his OS maps
model buses and acrylic paints
but charity shops accepted his unplayed games
(he'd never found another soul to play Diplomacy)
his unwatched films and unworn waistcoats.

The ukulele he'd never mastered,
the harmonica he rarely blew
and the guitar he cherished
he passed on to his grandchildren
along with teach-yourself manuals
a slide and a plastic plectrum.

He tried his damnedest to fix the broken garden seat,
the faulty flush and the dicky hinge
and even burnished a couple of fading friendships.
He erased any potential mysteries,
leaving no ambiguous poems,
no secret diaries, no stores of pills.

He left no debts, no regrets,
no animosity
and no unspoken love.

Pedlar's Halt

It was the secluded platform where they'd met,
not so much a station as a country stop.
Single line, small shelter, one wooden seat,
a name board spelling out Pedlar's Halt.

No human life, but everywhere
summer abundance, darting swallows,
a profusion of bees among the meadowsweet
and for a whole minute a blackbird singing.

She'd arrived early to savour the atmosphere
the expectation of illicit intimacy
the journey to the clifftop house
and maybe, this time, a promise...

At the appointed time, a figure approached
from the shadows of the trees... but not him,
a woman, a woman she'd seen before
in a photo in a wallet by a bedside.

Now the abundance seemed oppressive,
the seclusion, isolation.
And a patient hawk hovered
as a vole froze in the undergrowth.

She Lives

She lives, confined by four strong walls,
washed daily, rinsed, emptied;
everything well maintained, safety checked.
Her life is measured in pills and spoons,
samples, insulin, and Tramadol.
Briefly she glimpses the outside world,
a hint of light, a wayward sound,
but night shuts blinds, locks doors.

She dies, confined by four strong walls,
now washed, perfumed and plugged.
Offspring from afar sing praises:
so caring! so steadfast! so selfless!
The vicar pockets his fee with his principles
and measures her life with anecdotes.
The curtains close; she is whisked away
out of sight, out of mind, into dust.

She lives, confined in an album:
here, spruce in her schoolgirl uniform;
now showing a hen-night leg.
Oh, that's her man; well shot of him.
There, wearing a golden crown
she made for the Queen's Jubilee.
Ah, this is how we'll remember her,
with her kids in the park on a pedalo.

Long walk home

He chose to walk home from the surgery
taking the long way round despite the ice.
Along this less familiar way he noticed more –
the early blossoming of the blackthorn,
budding daffodils piercing the thin snow,
the glint of bare trees in the setting sun.
He sensed the waning power of winter
spring's insistent procreation,
life that will live on life,
ice preserving yet destroying
water quenching, drowning
the sun energising, cauterising
creation and destruction in equal measure
and he wondered at the terrible beauty
of his malignant cells multiplying.

Lights Out

She tells him to lie down
    get to sleep
    stop fussing.

She turns out the light
    closes the door
    leaves him.

Beneath the pillow
    his hidden torch
    and underneath

his bed a packed bag
    with outdoor shoes
    and some apple pie.

He lies waiting
    for the key in the door
    downstairs

and the shouting to start
    blaming him
    for their rift.

He vows to leave his
    mother's apron strings
    his father's

scorn and ridicule
    slip away
    silently

then work out
    how far it is
    to Bedfordshire

and whether there is a bus
    that will take him there
    for five pounds twenty.

Patient

Escorted by nurse and daughter
and connected to his catheter,
he slumps into his bedside chair.
He does not want to tell some nurse
whether or not his pains are worse;
nor will he commit himself
in this suspicious place
where food is forbidden
and toilets are under the bed.

"Doctors know what's best dad.
You need to talk. Let them know
how bad things are."
Summoned by shopping,
his daughter departs,
leaving him to the nurses' mercy.

He stays silent and stares all day.

Late at night, no nurses near,
holding his catheter
like some athlete's trophy,
he shuffles to the bed
of the bandaged man who never stirs.
"I'm going on holiday. This Friday. Blackpool.
With my daughter and her bloke.
Three star hotel. It's booked.
I might need a bit of help, though."

Bereft of response, he re-shuffles
and through until dawn he lies,
planning his great escape.

Allotment

Once the days left to him were specified,
he worked more intensely with the earth,
turning clay, breaking clods, raking fine tilth.
It helped him understand all that stuff
about dust unto dust. He thanked his
lucky stars he'd never had to make some
pointless sacrifice, beg or steal his meals,
shrink from persecution for his beliefs.

While he could grow his food from seed and breathe
sweet lavender, honeysuckle and stock
from the evening air, he did not need some
bucket list or luxury cruise. Simply
he sought to fade to black among his leeks
his cabbages and his blue hydrangeas.

Kursk

They travel in silence the two of them,
the train rattling northwards
through the deepening dark
and the encroaching snows.
Hope of a rescue flickers
like a tiny candle in a vast cathedral
but in their hearts they know
they've come to mourn.

There had been a birth
many years ago,
the one miracle in their mundane lives,
but now, both resurrection and creation
beyond them, they journey silently
the two of them.

Told to sit in an empty room,
with its unforgiving, fluorescent light,
they touch hands, helplessly,
like two castaways on a tiny island
above a bottomless sea.

Submerged in their sorrow,
they think of the desperation,
the suffocation, the deepsea grave,
not being there when most needed.

A phone rings relentlessly
in the empty office next door,
but no one comes to answer it...

Tough Times for Tiresias

"As flies to wanton boys are we to the gods – they kill us for their sport."
King Lear Act 4 scene I line 36

Easily enraged and keen to admonish
Not needing a reason to torment or punish
Old gods loved to trick and to tease us,
No wonder we welcomed the coming of Jesus.
Too late for poor young Tiresias though
Who came across, when out for a stroll,
Copulating snakes on Mount Cellene.
He was, of course, unwise to intervene.
He could have walked on, kept his nose in the air
But he grabbed the *in flagrante* pair,
Wrenched them apart, killing the female.
This was reported by some sad tell-tale
And the goddess Athena took up the case.
She had a bit of a thing concerning snakes;
Some she wore, on her cloak as a fringe
To make mere mortals shrink and cringe.
She was some tough cookie it has to be said
Born as she was from Zeus's split head:
Armed with spear and shield, she displayed
The skin of a giant she'd slain and flayed
As a breastplate in battle. She was ferocious,
So it seemed quite ironically preposterous
For her to be the goddess of embroidery!
When she heard of the snakecrime she went incendiary
And to stop Tiresias from further offending
She sentenced him to instant transgendering
Making him a woman right there on the spot

Which she thought was enough to teach him what's what,
But seven years later and Ms Tiresias,
Out for a stroll and minding her business,
Chanced upon two copulating snakes
And not having learned from past mistakes
She yanked them apart and killed the male,
Which to judgemental gods was beyond the pale.
Now you'd think that deities, being so resourceful,
Would respond with something especially forceful
Like throwing her into a pit full of vipers,
But what do they do, just go and re-type her:
He's a man again!
        Now the gods' omniscience
Is no more omni than your average adolescent's
And it seems that as far as sex goes
They are so naïve that they suppose
That s/he, knowing both sorts of ardour,
Is fit to become a sexual counsellor
Pronouncing on what's OK and what's improper;
But this is where Big T comes a cropper;
When Hera, wife of Zeus, hears the answer
To the simple question, 'Who gets most pleasure
The man or the woman? Tell it straight.'
'It's women,' says Big T, 'by two to eight.'
This makes Hera so damned irate
She strikes Tiresias blind, which fate
Probably turned him into an atheist.

Everything wasn't black though and Zeus,
Thinking that Tiresias had had it too tough,
Gives him the power of foresight, just enough
For him to become a top soothsayer -
'He can't see the present but can see the future!'
If only he'd had that gift from the start
He might not have upset the whole applecart.
So if you should see some ophidian coitus
Don't ever try any kind of interruptus.

End room

The security door closes behind us
and the cheerful nurse leads the way
through the hazards of the corridor
the threats, the offers, the fondling...
Sex is the last drive to go you know
...the pleading and the protestations
past the rooms with the bedbound
the empty eyed, the drugged
past the unused equipment
of the Activity Room
We're a bit short staffed at the mo
through the common room
with its forced joviality
desperate matiness
the staff counting the hours
more bemused than the patients
searching for glimmers of sense
longing for some kind of connection
until we reach the end room
triangular, bare
save for a painting
of a garden in summer
with pink roses and some honeysuckle
climbing a secluded arbour
with its unoccupied wooden chair.
There beneath the painting
crouches Rosalind, head bowed,

rocking back and forth, mumbling...
I think it's poetry.
It's about a hive for a honey bee.
Your husband's come to see you Rosie,
isn't that lovely?

Sea Rocket

Hardy, resourceful and unpretentious
it settles on barren shores, in tangled heaps
of stranded kelp, seaweed embankments,

binding unstable sand with strong taproots.
Its seaborne seeds the first to germinate
on Surtsey's new-born volcanic strand.

Buoyant and waterproof, its seedpods
are whisked away by winds
and swept by coastal currents

to find tight bays where surf is strong,
landing when tides are highest
as earth, moon and sun align.

When threatened by windblown sand
it does not shrink but grows taller.
It resists disease, withstands pollution,

can disappear for years and be born again
or travel the world in ships' ballast,
a considerate visitor, never invader.

And when we blundering apes
have burned and drowned ourselves
or absconded into space

this resilient, transient plant
will still bloom on till doomsday
on whatever scraps of shore survive.